AIR F[RYER]

cookbook

The complete air fryer recipe book,
a smart way to cook quick and
healthy meals

TABLE OF CONTENTS

INTRODUCTION

Why Air Fryers Were Invented and Why They Remain Popular

It may surprise people to know that the first air fryers weren't introduced into the market until 2010. That means that air frying technology is younger than the iPhone. The home-use technology was invented for two very important reasons. One, air fryers are a much healthier way to create the same crispy on the outside/soft on the inside food that traditional frying in oil creates. The second reason is that they are a fast and convenient way to cook for the entire family.

How Air Fryers Deliver Delicious Foods with a Fraction of the Grease

So how do air fryers manage to make their magic? The answer lies in their interesting design that has a heating element on one end and a fan on the other. The fan circulates super-hot air around the food, cooking it from the outside in and creating the same effect (called the Maillard effect) that you get with fried foods. The difference is that instead of using fat-filled oils, you are using calorie-free air. Many recipes still call for a little oil, but it is literally a fraction of a percentage of what you would use with the traditional frying method.

Make Meals for Any Occasion

This is an overlooked benefit of the air fryer and one that I think deserves a little more attention. Again, this machine is not just for potatoes and chicken; it can be used to cook anything from breakfast to desserts. To take that idea one step further, thanks to its safety and versatility air fryers like this one can be used to cook for any occasion. It is great to fry up multiple courses for a cookout or leave something warming on the counter in a busy house during Thanksgiving.

Enjoyed by Everyone from College Kids to Professional Chefs

As noted, professional chefs love to use air fryers because of their many benefits, but you don't have to be a pro to use this machine like one. It's not just for busy moms and dads who don't have much time to cook for the family. Air fryers like this one are becoming increasingly popular with college kids because they are so easy to use, make great tasting food, and are safe enough for a dorm room.

Much Healthier Than Traditional Fryers Preserving Nutrients, Using Less Oil and Fewer Carbs

One of the best reasons to own an air fryer is that you don't need to fry your foods in a pool of fatty oil. You get all of the taste and texture of fried foods without having the calories and guilt that come along with traditional fried foods. Additionally, foods cooked in an air fryer hold their nutrients better to make them just as healthy as they are mouthwatering. The best part is that you get all of these benefits without having to sacrifice portion size or taste.

BREAKFAST

Cheesy Melted Stuffed Tomatoes

Preparation Time: 5 Minutes

Cooking Time: 25 Minutes

Servings: 4

Ingredients:

- 1 lb. large red tomatoes
- 2 tablespoons extra virgin olive oil
- ½ cup ground chicken
- 1-tablespoon chopped shallots
- 1-teaspoon minced garlic
- 1-teaspoon oregano
- ½ teaspoon dried mint
- 2 tablespoons crumbled feta cheese
- 2 tablespoons ground pine nuts
- ¾ cup grated mozzarella cheese

Directions:

1. Season the ground chicken with shallots, garlic, oregano, and dried mints then mix well.
2. Add ground pine nuts and feta cheese to the chicken mixture then mix until just combined. Set aside.
3. Cut the tomatoes into halves then discard the seeds.
4. Fill each halved tomato with the chicken mixture then sprinkle grated mozzarella cheese on top.
5. Next, install the crisper plate and preheat the Ninja Foodi for 3 minutes.
6. Select the "Bake" menu then set the temperature to 325°F and set the time to 15 minutes.
7. Arrange the stuffed tomatoes in the Ninja Foodi's basket then press the "Start/Stop" button to begin. Bake the stuffed tomatoes.

8. Once the Ninja Foodi beeps take the stuffed tomatoes with melted mozzarella on top out of the Ninja Foodi and transfer them to a serving dish.
9. Serve and enjoy.

Nutrition: 229 Calories, 17.7g Fats, 4.6g Net Carbs, 13.1g Protein

Butternut Squash Creamy Lemon

Preparation Time: 5 Minutes
Cooking Time: 25 Minutes
Servings: 4

Ingredients:

- 1 lb. butternut squash
- 1-tablespoon extra-virgin olive oil
- 2 tablespoons butter
- 1-teaspoon minced garlic
- A pinch of salt
- A pinch of pepper
- ¼ cup Greek yogurt
- 2 tablespoons sour cream
- 1-tablespoon lemon juice
- ½ teaspoon diced mint leaves

Directions:

1. Cut the butternut squash into cubes then set aside.
2. Install the crisper plate and preheat the Ninja Foodi for 3 minutes.
3. Select the "Air Roast" menu then set the temperature to 375°F and set the time to 12 minutes.
4. Spread the butternut squash cubes in the Ninja Foodi's basket then spray olive oil over them.
5. Press the "Start/Stop" button to begin then air roast the butternut squash.

---

6. Once it is done, quickly transfer the roasted butternut squash to a mixing bowl then add butter, salt, and pepper.
7. Toss well then using an immersion blender blend the roasted butternut squash until becoming puree.
8. Transfer the butternut squash puree to a serving bowl then set aside.
9. Next, place the Greek yogurt together with sour cream, lemon juice, and diced mint leaves then blend them until smooth and incorporated.
10. Drizzle the creamy sauce over the butternut squash puree then serve.
11. Enjoy!

Nutrition: 142 Calories, 13.2g Fats, 3.7g Net Carbs, 1.7g Protein

Spinach Egg Muffins with Bacon

Preparation Time: 5 Minutes
Cooking Time: 25 Minutes
Servings: 4

Ingredients:

- 4 eggs
- 2 tablespoons heavy cream
- ¼ teaspoon salt
- ¼ teaspoon pepper
- 3 tablespoons diced onion
- ¼ cup chopped spinach
- ½ cup grated cheddar cheese
- 2 slices bacon
- 3 tablespoons grated mozzarella cheese

Directions:

1. Cut the bacon into crumbles then set aside.
2. Crack the eggs then mix them with heavy cream.
3. Season the eggs with salt and pepper then stir until incorporated.
4. Add diced onion, chopped spinach, crumbled bacon, and grated cheddar cheese to the egg mixture then stir until combined.
5. Next, install the crisper plate and preheat the Ninja Foodi for 3 minutes.
6. Select the "Bake" menu then set the temperature to 300°F and set the time to 15 minutes.
7. Pour the egg mixture into several silicone molds then drizzle mozzarella cheese on top.
8. Insert the molds into the Ninja Foodi's basket then press the "Start/Stop" button to begin. Bake the egg muffins.

9. Once the Ninja Foodi beeps and the egg muffins are done, remove them from the Ninja Foodi and let them cool.
10. Take the egg muffins out of the molds then arrange them on a serving dish.
11. Serve and enjoy.

Nutrition: 201 Calories, 16.1g Fats, 1.5g Net Carbs, 12.6g Protein

Cheesy Mozzarella Pumpkin Casserole

Preparation Time: 5 Minutes
Cooking Time: 25 Minutes
Servings: 4

Ingredients:

- 2 cups pumpkin cubes
- 2 teaspoons minced garlic
- ½ cup mayonnaise
- ¼ cup of coconut milk
- ¼ teaspoon salt
- ¼ teaspoon pepper
- ¾ tablespoon diced thyme
- ¼ teaspoon cinnamon
- ½ cup grated mozzarella cheese
- 2 tablespoons diced celeries

Directions:

1. Prepare a casserole dish that fits into the Ninja Foodi's basket then spread the pumpkin cubes in it.
2. Combine mayonnaise with coconut milk then season it with minced garlic, salt, pepper, and thyme. Stir until incorporated.
3. Pour the sauce mixture over the pumpkin cubes then sprinkle grated mozzarella cheese and cinnamon on top. Set aside.

4. Next, install the crisper plate and preheat the Ninja Foodi for 3 minutes.
5. Select the "Bake" menu then set the temperature to 375°F and set the time to 20 minutes.
6. Insert the casserole dish into the Ninja Foodi's basket then press the "Start/Stop" button to begin. Bake the pumpkin casserole.
7. Once the Ninja Foodi beeps and the pumpkin casserole is done, remove it from the Ninja Foodi and sprinkle diced celeries on top.
8. Serve and enjoy.

Nutrition: 242 Calories, 21.4g Fats, 5.8g Net Carbs, 7.3g Protein

Mushroom Veggie Frittata with Ricotta Cheese

Preparation Time: 5 Minutes
Cooking Time: 25 Minutes
Servings: 4

Ingredients:

- 4 eggs
- 1-tablespoon coconut oil
- ¾ cup unsweetened almond milk
- ¼ teaspoon salt
- ½ teaspoon pepper
- ½ cup ricotta cheese
- 2 slices bacon
- 1-cup broccoli florets
- ½ cup chopped mushroom
- ½ cup diced red tomatoes

Directions:

1. Prepare a casserole dish that fits into the Ninja Foodi's basket then coat it with coconut oil. Set aside.
2. Crack the eggs then place them in a bowl.
3. Pour almond milk into the eggs then season the mixture with salt and pepper. Stir until incorporated.
4. Cut the bacon into small dices then add them to the egg mixture together with ricotta cheese, broccoli florets, mushrooms, and red tomatoes. Mix well.
5. Transfer the egg mixture to the prepared casserole dish then spread evenly.
6. Next, install the crisper plate and preheat the Ninja Foodi for 3 minutes.

7. Select the "Bake" menu then set the temperature to 360°F and set the time to 20 minutes.
8. Insert the casserole dish into the Ninja Foodi's basket then press the "Start/Stop" button to begin. Bake the frittata.
9. Once the Ninja Foodi beeps and the frittata is done, remove it from the Ninja Foodi and serve.
10.   Enjoy!

Nutrition: 228 Calories, 17.8g Fats, 4.1g Net Carbs, 12.6g Protein

Breaded Green Bell Pepper Fritter with Sesame Seeds (Vegan)

Preparation Time: 5 Minutes
Cooking Time: 25 Minutes
Servings: 4
Ingredients:

- 1 lb. green bell peppers
- ¼ cup diced onion
- 3 tablespoons almond flour
- ¼ teaspoon salt
- 1-teaspoon minced garlic
- ½ teaspoon chili powder
- ¼ teaspoon pepper
- 2 eggs
- 1-cup pecan crumbles
- 2 tablespoons sesame seeds
- 1-tablespoon extra-virgin olive oil

Directions:

1. Cut the bell peppers into cubes then place them in a food processor. Process them until becoming crumbles.
2. Add diced onion, almond flour, and an egg to the bell pepper crumbles then season it with salt, minced garlic, chili powder, and pepper. Mix well.
3. Divide the mixture into 8 then shape each part into a fritter form.

4. Arrange the fritters in a container then freeze them for at least 2 hours. After 2 hours, take the bell pepper fritters out of the freezer.
5. Crack the remaining egg and place it in a bowl. Whisk until incorporated.
6. Take a bell pepper fritter then dip it in the beaten egg and roll it in the pecan crumbles. Repeat with the remaining fritters.
7. Next, install the crisper plate and preheat the Ninja Foodi for 3 minutes.
8. Select the "Air Fry" menu then set the temperature to 360°F and set the time to 8 minutes.
9. Arrange the bell pepper fritters in the Ninja Foodi's basket then baste egg over the fritters.
10. Sprinkle sesame seeds on top then press the "Start/Stop" button to begin. Fry the bell pepper fritters.
11. Once the Ninja Foodi beeps and the bell pepper fritters are done, take them out of the Ninja Foodi and arrange them on a serving dish. Repeat with the remaining bell pepper fritters.
12. Serve and enjoy.

Nutrition: 160 Calories, 13.8g Fats, 5.9g Net Carbs, 5.1g Protein

Nutty Berry Granola with Coconut Flakes

Preparation Time: 5 Minutes
Cooking Time: 10 Minutes
Servings: 4

Ingredients:

- ¼ cup chopped almonds
- ¼ cup chopped hazelnuts
- ½ cup chopped pecans
- 2 tablespoons pumpkin seeds
- 1-tablespoon sunflower seeds
- 1-tablespoon flax seed
- 2 tablespoons coconut flakes
- 1 egg white
- 1-tablespoon butter
- 1-½ cups almond milk
- 1 cup fresh berries, as you desired

Directions:

1. Combine the entire ingredients except for almond milk and ground cinnamon in a food processor then mix well.
2. Install the crisper plate and preheat the Ninja Foodi for 3 minutes.
3. Select the "Air Roast" menu then set the temperature to 350°F and set the time to 8 minutes.
4. Spread the nut mixture in the Ninja Foodi's basket then press the "Start/Stop" button to begin. Roast the nut mixture.
5. Once the Ninja Foodi beeps and the granola is done, remove them from the Ninja Foodi and transfer them to a serving bowl. Let it cool.

6. To serve, pour almond milk over the granola then sprinkle on top.
7. Enjoy.

Nutrition: 311 Calories, 28.2g Fats, 6.9g Net Carbs, 6.3g Protein

Spinach Mushroom Quiche with Cheese

Preparation Time: 5 Minutes
Cooking Time: 25 Minutes
Servings: 4

Ingredients:

- ¼ cup butter
- ½ cup almond flour
- 1 egg yolk
- 4 eggs
- 2 tablespoons heavy cream
- 2 tablespoons unsweetened almond milk
- ¼ cup chopped spinach
- 2 tablespoons diced mushroom
- ½ cup cheddar cheese cubes

Directions:

1. Prepare a baking pan that fits into the Ninja Foodi then coat with cooking spray.
2. Place butter in a mixing bowl then add the egg yolk and almond flour to it.
3. Using a pastry knife, mix the ingredients until becoming dough then place it on a flat surface.
4. Using a rolling pin press the dough until becoming a thin layer then apply it onto the prepared pan. Using a fork prick the crust.
5. Install the crisper plate and broil rack into the basket of your Ninja Foodi then place the pan with crust on the boil rack.

6. Select the "Bake" menu and cook the crust at 375°F for 3 minutes.
7. In the meantime, crack the eggs then place them in a mixing bowl.
8. Add heavy cream and almond milk to the eggs and whisk them until incorporated.
9. Stir in the chopped spinach, diced mushrooms, and cheese cubes to the egg mixture then mix until combined.
10. Pour the egg mixture into the aluminum foil with crust and spread it evenly.
11. Select the "Bake" menu again and cook the quiche at 350°F for 20 minutes.
12. Once it is done, take the quiche out of your Ninja Foodi and serve.
13. Enjoy!

Nutrition: 283 Calories, 26.2g Fats, 1.3g Net Carbs, 10.9g Protein

Avocado Lettuce Salads in Crispy Rolls (Vegan)

Preparation Time: 5 Minutes
Cooking Time: 15 Minutes
Servings: 4

Ingredients:

- ½ cup almond flour
- 2 tablespoons coconut flour
- ¼ teaspoon salt
- ¼ teaspoon pepper
- 2-½ tablespoons coconut oil
- 3 tablespoons coconut milk
- ¾ cup avocado cubes
- ½ cup chopped onion
- ½ cup chopped lettuce
- 3 tablespoons mayonnaise
- 2 tablespoons lemon juice
- 2 tablespoons extra virgin olive oil

Directions:

1. Combine the almond flour with coconut flour then season it with salt and pepper.
2. Pour avocado oil over the flour then knead it until becoming dough. Add a tablespoon of coconut milk one at a time, if it is necessary.
3. Using a rolling pin press the dough into a thin layer then using a mold cut the layer into 8-inch circles. Set aside.
4. Combine the avocado cubes with diced onion then drizzle lemon juice over them. Toss to season.
5. After that, take a sheet of thin dough and place it on a flat surface.
6. Arrange fresh lettuce on the thin dough then spread the avocado and onion salad on it.

7. Drizzle mayonnaise on top then roll the dough until the salads are completely wrapped. Repeat with the remaining dough and salads.
8. Next, install the crisper plate into the basket of your Ninja Foodi then preheat the Ninja Foodi for 3 minutes.
9. Select the "Bake" menu then set the temperature to 375°F and adjust the time to 5 minutes.
10. Arrange the stuffed rolls in the Ninja Foodi's basket then spray olive oil over them.
11. Press the "Start/Stop" button to begin then bake the crispy rolls.
12. Once the Ninja Foodi beeps, take the rolls out of the Ninja Foodi and arrange them to a serving dish.
13. Serve and enjoy.

Nutrition: 344 Calories, 33.5g Fats, 4.7g Net Carbs, 2.8g Protein

Zucchini Pancakes with Mayo Garlic Sauce

Preparation Time: 5 Minutes
Cooking Time: 25 Minutes
Servings: 4

Ingredients:

- 1 lb. medium zucchinis
- ½ teaspoon salt
- ¼ cup almond flour
- 3 tablespoons grated Parmesan cheese
- 1 egg
- 2 tablespoons extra virgin olive oil
- 3 tablespoons mayonnaise
- ½ cup sour cream
- ½ teaspoon garlic powder
- ¼ teaspoon pepper
- ¼ teaspoon dried parsley
- ¼ teaspoon dried tarragon
- ¼ teaspoon minced dill
- ¼ teaspoon paprika

Directions:

1. Cut the zucchinis into halves lengthwise then discard the seeds.
2. Using a julienne peeler cut the zucchinis into noodle form then mix it with salt, almond flour, grated Parmesan cheese, and egg. Mix well.
3. Divide the zucchini mixture into 8 then shape each part into a pancake form. Set aside.

---

4. Next, install the crisper plate into the basket of your Ninja Foodi then preheat the Ninja Foodi for 3 minutes.
5. Select the "Air Fry" menu then set the temperature to 360°F and adjust the time to 5 minutes.
6. Arrange the zucchini pancakes in the Ninja Foodi's basket then spray olive oil over them.
7. Press the "Start/Stop" button to begin then fry the zucchini pancakes.
8. Once the Ninja Foodi beeps and the zucchini pancakes are done, take them out of the Ninja Foodi and transfer them to a serving dish. Repeat with the remaining zucchini pancakes.
9. In the meantime, combine mayonnaise with sour cream then season the mixture with garlic powder, pepper, parsley, tarragon, dill, and paprika. Stir until incorporated.
10. Serve the zucchini pancakes with the mayo sauce and vegetables then enjoy it.

Nutrition: 260 Calories, 24.2g Fats, 4.3g Net Carbs, 6.1g Protein

LUNCH

Meatballs

Preparation Time: 10 minutes
Cooking Time: 12 minutes
Serve: 4

Ingredients:

- 4 oz ground lamb
- 1/2 tbsp lemon zest
- 1 egg, lightly beaten
- 1 tbsp oregano, chopped
- 1/4 tsp dried thyme
- Pepper
- Salt

Directions:

1. Spray air fryer basket with cooking spray.
2. Add all ingredients into the bowl and mix until well combined.
3. Make meatballs from mixture and place into the air fryer basket and cook at 400 F for 12 minutes.
4. Serve and enjoy.

Nutrition: Calories 73 Fat 3.3 g Carbohydrates 1 g Sugar 0.2 g Protein 9.5 g Cholesterol 66 mg

Garlic Herb Lamb Cutlets

Preparation Time: 10 minutes
Cooking Time: 30 minutes
Servings: 4

Ingredients:

- 4 lamb cutlets
- 1/2 tbsp chives, chopped
- 2 tbsp mustard
- 2 garlic cloves, minced
- 1/2 tbsp oregano, chopped
- 1/2 tbsp basil, chopped
- 1 tsp olive oil
- Pepper
- Salt

Directions:

1. Spray air fryer basket with cooking spray.
2. Add lamb cutlets into the bowl with remaining ingredients and coat well.
3. Place lamb cutlets into the air fryer basket and cook at 380 F for 30 minutes. Turn lamb cutlets halfway through.
4. Serve and enjoy.

Nutrition: Calories 199 Fat 9.1 g Carbohydrates 2.9 g Sugar 0.4 g Protein 25.5 g Cholesterol 77 mg

Spicy Lamb Chops

Preparation Time: 10 minutes
Cooking Time: 20 minutes
Servings: 4
Ingredients:
- 4 lamb chops
- 1/2 tsp chili powder
- 1 tbsp garlic, minced
- 1 tbsp olive oil
- 1/4 tsp paprika
- 1/4 tsp cayenne
- Pepper
- Salt

Directions:
1. Add lamb chops into the bowl with remaining ingredients and coat well.
2. Place lamb chops into the air fryer basket and cook at 390 F for 20 minutes. Turn lamb chops halfway through.
3. Serve and enjoy.

Nutrition: Calories 193 Fat 9.8 g Carbohydrates 1 g Sugar 0.1 g Protein 24.1 g Cholesterol 77 mg

Greek Lamb Patties

Preparation Time: 10 minutes
Cooking Time: 20 minutes
Servings: 4

Ingredients:

- 1 1/2 lbs. ground lamb
- 1/3 cup feta cheese, crumbled
- 1 tsp oregano
- 1/4 tsp Italian seasoning
- 1/4 tsp pepper
- 1/2 tsp salt

Directions:

1. Preheat the cosori air fryer to 375 F.
2. Add all ingredients into the bowl and mix until well combined.
3. Make four equal shape of patties from meat mixture and place into the air fryer basket.
4. Cook patties for 20 minutes. Turn patties halfway through.
5. Serve and enjoy.

Nutrition: Calories 352 Fat 15.3 g Carbohydrates 0.9 g Sugar 0.6 g Protein 49.6 g Cholesterol 164 mg

Mustard Lamb Chops

Preparation Time: 10 minutes
Cooking Time: 15 minutes
Servings: 4

Ingredients:

- 8 lamb chops
- 1/2 tsp olive oil
- 1 1/2 tbsp Dijon mustard
- 1 1/2 tbsp fresh lemon juice
- Pepper
- Salt

Directions:

1. Preheat the cosori air fryer to 390 F.
2. In a small bowl, mix together mustard, lemon juice, and olive oil.
3. Brush lamb chops with mustard mixture and place into the air fryer basket.
4. Cook lamb chops for 15 minutes. Turn halfway through.
5. Serve and enjoy.

Nutrition: Calories 327 Fat 13.3 g Carbohydrates 0.5 g Sugar 0.2 g Protein 48.1 g Cholesterol 153 mg

Pork Taquitos

Preparation Time: 10 minutes
Cooking Time: 16 minutes
Servings: 8

Ingredients:

- 1 juiced lime
- 10 whole wheat tortillas
- 2 ½ C. shredded mozzarella cheese
- 30 ounces of cooked and shredded pork tenderloin

Directions:

1. Preparing the Ingredients. Ensure your air fryer is preheated to 380 degrees.
2. Drizzle pork with lime juice and gently mix.
3. Heat up tortillas in the microwave with a dampened paper towel to soften.
4. Add about 3 ounces of pork and ¼ cup of shredded cheese to each tortilla. Tightly roll them up.
5. Spray the Cosori air fryer basket with a bit of olive oil.
6. Air Frying. Set temperature to 380°F, and set time to 10 minutes. Air fry taquitos 7-10 minutes till tortillas turn a slight golden color, making sure to flip halfway through cooking process.

Nutrition: Calories: 309Fat: 11gProtein: 21gSugar: 2g

Cajun Bacon Pork Loin Fillet

Preparation Time: 10 minutes + 1 hour marination
Cooking Time: 20 minutes
Servings: 6

Ingredients:

- 1½ pounds pork loin fillet or pork tenderloin
- 3 tablespoons olive oil
- 2 tablespoons Cajun Spice Mix
- Salt
- 6 slices bacon
- Olive oil spray

Directions:

1. Preparing the Ingredients. Cut the pork in half so that it will fit in the air fryer basket.
2. Place both pieces of meat in a resealable plastic bag. Add the oil, Cajun seasoning, and salt to taste, if using. Seal the bag and massage to coat all of the meat with the oil and seasonings. Marinate in the refrigerator for at least 1 hour or up to 24 hours.
3. Air Frying. Remove the pork from the bag and wrap 3 bacon slices around each piece. Spray the Cosori air fryer basket with olive oil spray. Place the meat in the air fryer. Set the Cosori air fryer to 350°F for 15 minutes. Increase the temperature to 400°F for 5 minutes. Use a meat thermometer to ensure the meat has reached an internal temperature of 145°F.
4. Let the meat rest for 10 minutes. Slice into 6 medallions and serve.

Nutrition: Calories: 309 Fat: 11g Protein: 21g Sugar: 2g

Panko-Breaded Pork Chops

Preparation Time: 5 minutes
Cooking Time: 17 minutes
Servings: 6

Ingredients

- 5 (3½- to 5-ounce) pork chops (bone-in or boneless)
- Seasoning salt
- Pepper
- ¼ cup all-purpose flour
- 2 tablespoons panko bread crumbs
- Cooking oil

Directions:

1. Preparing the Ingredients. Season the pork chops with the seasoning salt and pepper to taste.
2. Sprinkle the flour on both sides of the pork chops, then coat both sides with panko bread crumbs.
3. Place the pork chops in the air fryer. Stacking them is okay.
4. Air Frying. Spray the pork chops with cooking oil. Cook for 6 minutes.
5. Open the Air fryer and flip the pork chops. Cook for an additional 6 minutes
6. Cool before serving.
7. Typically, bone-in pork chops are juicier than boneless. If you prefer really juicy pork chops, use bone-in.

Nutrition: Calories: 246 Fat: 13g Protein: 26g Fiber: 0g

Porchetta-Style Pork Chops

Preparation Time: 15 minutes
Cooking Time: 25 minutes
Servings: 2

Ingredients

- 1 tablespoon extra-virgin olive oil
- Grated zest of 1 lemon
- 2 cloves garlic, minced
- 2 teaspoons chopped fresh rosemary
- 1 teaspoon finely chopped fresh sage
- 1 teaspoon fennel seeds, lightly crushed
- ¼ to ½ teaspoon red pepper flakes
- 1 teaspoon kosher salt
- 1 teaspoon black pepper
- (8-ounce) center-cut bone-in pork chops, about 1 inch thick

Directions:

1. Preparing the Ingredients. In a small bowl, combine the olive oil, zest, garlic, rosemary, sage, fennel seeds, red pepper, salt, and black pepper. Stir, crushing the herbs with the back of a spoon, until a paste form. Spread the seasoning mix on both sides of the pork chops.
2. Air Frying. Place the chops in the air fryer basket. Set the Cosori air fryer to 375°F for 15 minutes. Use a meat thermometer to ensure the chops have reached an internal temperature of 145°F.

Nutrition: Calories: 246 Fat: 13g Protein: 26g Fiber: 0g

Apricot Glazed Pork Tenderloins

Preparation Time: 5 minutes
Cooking Time: 30 minutes
Servings: 3

Ingredients

- 1 teaspoon salt
- 1/2 teaspoon pepper
- 1-lb pork tenderloin
- 2 tablespoons minced fresh rosemary or 1 tablespoon dried rosemary, crushed
- 2 tablespoons olive oil, divided
- 1 garlic clove, minced
- Apricot Glaze Ingredients
- 1 cup apricot preserves
- 3 garlic cloves, minced
- 4 tablespoons lemon juice

Directions:

1. Preparing the Ingredients. Mix well pepper, salt, garlic, oil, and rosemary. Brush all over pork. If needed cut pork crosswise in half to fit in air fryer. Lightly grease baking pan of air fryer with cooking spray. Add pork.
2. Air Frying. For 3 minutes per side, brown pork in a preheated 390°F air fryer. Meanwhile, mix well all glaze Ingredients in a small bowl. Baste pork every 5 minutes. Cook for 20 minutes at 330°F. Serve and enjoy.

Nutrition: Calories: 246 Fat: 13g Protein: 26g Fiber: 0g

DINNER

Crispy Chicken Tenders

Preparation Time: 10 Minutes
Cooking Time: 15 Minutes
Servings: 4

Ingredients:
- 1 cup panko bread crumbs
- 1 tablespoon paprika
- ½ teaspoon salt
- ¼ teaspoon freshly ground black pepper
- 16 chicken tenders
- ½ cup mayonnaise
- Olive oil spray

Directions:
1. In a medium bowl, stir together the panko, paprika, salt, and pepper.
2. In a large bowl, toss together the chicken tenders and mayonnaise to coat. Transfer the coated chicken pieces to the bowl of seasoned panko and dredge to coat thoroughly. Press the coating onto the chicken with your fingers.
3. Insert the crisper plate into the basket and the basket into the unit. Preheat the unit by selecting AIR FRY, setting the temperature to 350°F, and setting the time to 3 minutes. Select START/STOP to begin.
4. Once the unit is preheated, place a parchment paper liner into the basket. Place the chicken into the basket and spray it with olive oil.
5. Select AIR FRY, set the temperature to 350°F, and set the time to 15 minutes. Select START/STOP to begin.

---

6. When the cooking is complete, the tenders will be golden brown and a food thermometer inserted into the chicken should register 165°F. For more even browning, remove the basket halfway through cooking and flip the tenders. Give them an extra spray of olive oil and reinsert the basket to resume cooking. This ensures they are crispy and brown all over.
7. When the cooking is complete, serve.

Nutrition: Calories: 377; Total fat: 22g; Saturated fat: 3g; Cholesterol: 73mg; Sodium: 799mg; Carbohydrates: 18g; Fiber: 1g; Protein: 28g

Chicken Cordon Bleu

Preparation Time: 15 Minutes
Cooking Time: 15 Minutes
Servings: 4

Ingredients:
- 4 chicken breast filets
- ¼ cup chopped ham
- 1/3 cup grated Swiss cheese, or Gruyere cheese
- ¼ cup all-purpose flour
- Pinch salt
- Freshly ground black pepper
- ½ teaspoon dried marjoram
- 1 egg
- 1 cup panko bread crumbs
- Olive oil spray

Directions:
1. Put the chicken breast filets on a work surface and gently press them with the palm of your hand to make them a bit thinner. Don't tear the meat.
2. In a small bowl, combine the ham and cheese. Divide this mixture among the chicken filets. Wrap the chicken around the filling to enclose it, using toothpicks to hold the chicken together.
3. In a shallow bowl, stir together the flour, salt, pepper, and marjoram.
4. In another bowl, beat the egg.
5. Spread the panko on a plate.

6. Dip the chicken in the flour mixture, in the egg, and in the panko to coat thoroughly. Press the crumbs into the chicken so they stick well.
7. Insert the crisper plate into the basket and the basket into the unit. Preheat the unit by selecting BAKE, setting the temperature to 375°F, and setting the time to 3 minutes. Select START/STOP to begin.
8. Once the unit is preheated, spray the crisper plate with olive oil. Place the chicken into the basket and spray it with olive oil.
9. Select BAKE, set the temperature to 375°F, and set the time to 15 minutes. Select START/STOP to begin.
10.   When the cooking is complete, the chicken should be cooked through and a food thermometer inserted into the chicken should register 165°F. Carefully remove the toothpicks and serve.

Nutrition: Calories: 478; Total fat: 12g; Saturated fat: 3g; Cholesterol: 200mg; Sodium: 575mg; Carbohydrates: 26g; Fiber: 2g; Protein: 64g

Spicy Air-Crisped Chicken and Potatoes

Preparation Time: 5 Minutes
Cooking Time: 25 Minutes
Servings: 4

Ingredients:
- 4 bone-in, skin-on chicken thighs
- ½ teaspoon kosher salt or ¼ teaspoon fine salt
- 2 tablespoons melted unsalted butter
- 2 teaspoons Worcestershire sauce
- 2 teaspoons curry powder
- 1 teaspoon dried oregano leaves
- ½ teaspoon dry mustard
- ½ teaspoon granulated garlic
- ¼ teaspoon paprika
- ¼ teaspoon hot pepper sauce, such as Tabasco
- Cooking oil spray
- 4 medium Yukon gold potatoes, chopped
- 1 tablespoon extra-virgin olive oil

Directions:
1. Sprinkle the chicken thighs on both sides with salt.
2. In a medium bowl, stir together the melted butter, Worcestershire sauce, curry powder, oregano, dry mustard, granulated garlic, paprika, and hot pepper sauce. Add the thighs to the sauce and stir to coat.

3. Insert the crisper plate into the basket and the basket into the unit. Preheat the unit by selecting AIR FRY, setting the temperature to 400°F, and setting the time to 3 minutes. Select START/STOP to begin.

4. Once the unit is preheated, spray the crisper plate with cooking oil. In the basket, combine the potatoes and olive oil and toss to coat.

5. Add the wire rack to the air fryer and place the chicken thighs on top.

6. Select AIR FRY, set the temperature to 400°F, and set the time to 25 minutes. Select START/STOP to begin.

7. After 19 minutes check the chicken thighs. If a food thermometer inserted into the chicken registers 165°F, transfer them to a clean plate, and cover with aluminum foil to keep warm. If they aren't cooked to 165°F, resume cooking for another 1 to 2 minutes until they are done. Remove them from the unit along with the rack.

8. Remove the basket and shake it to distribute the potatoes. Reinsert the basket to resume cooking for 3 to 6 minutes, or until the potatoes are crisp and golden brown.

9. When the cooking is complete, serve the chicken with the potatoes.

Nutrition: Calories: 333; Total fat: 14g; Saturated fat: 5g; Cholesterol: 109mg; Sodium: 428mg; Carbohydrates: 27g; Fiber: 3g; Protein: 25g

Buttermilk Fried Chicken

Preparation Time: 7 Minutes
Cooking Time: 20 to 25 Minutes
Servings: 4

Ingredients:

- 1 cup all-purpose flour
- 2 teaspoons paprika
- Pinch salt
- Freshly ground black pepper
- 1/3 cup buttermilk
- 2 eggs
- 2 tablespoons extra-virgin olive oil
- 1½ cups bread crumbs
- 6 chicken pieces, drumsticks, breasts, and thighs, patted dry
- Cooking oil spray

Directions:

1. In a shallow bowl, stir together the flour, paprika, salt, and pepper.
2. In another bowl, beat the buttermilk and eggs until smooth.
3. In a third bowl, stir together the olive oil and bread crumbs until mixed.
4. Dredge the chicken in the flour, dip in the eggs to coat, and finally press into the bread crumbs, patting the crumbs firmly onto the chicken skin.
5. Insert the crisper plate into the basket and the basket into the unit. Preheat the unit by selecting AIR FRY, setting the temperature to 375°F, and setting the time to 3 minutes. Select START/STOP to begin.

6. Once the unit is preheated, spray the crisper plate with cooking oil. Place the chicken into the basket.
7. Select AIR FRY, set the temperature to 375°F, and set the time to 25 minutes. Select START/STOP to begin.
8. After 10 minutes, flip the chicken. Resume cooking. After 10 minutes more, check the chicken. If a food thermometer inserted into the chicken registers 165°F and the chicken is brown and crisp, it is done. Otherwise, resume cooking for up to 5 minutes longer.
9. When the cooking is complete, let cool for 5 minutes, then serve.

Nutrition: Calories: 644; Total fat: 17g; Saturated fat: 4g; Cholesterol: 214mg; Sodium: 495mg; Carbohydrates: 55g; Fiber: 3g; Protein: 62g

Korean Chicken Wings

Preparation Time: 10 Minutes
Cooking Time: 25 Minutes
Servings: 4
Ingredients:
- ¼ cup gochujang, or red pepper paste
- ¼ cup mayonnaise
- 2 tablespoons honey
- 1 tablespoon sesame oil
- 2 teaspoons minced garlic
- 1 tablespoon sugar
- 2 teaspoons ground ginger
- 3 pounds whole chicken wings
- Olive oil spray
- 1 teaspoon salt
- ½ teaspoon freshly ground black pepper

Directions:
1. In a large bowl, whisk the gochujang, mayonnaise, honey, sesame oil, garlic, sugar, and ginger. Set aside.
2. Insert the crisper plate into the basket and the basket into the unit. Preheat the unit by selecting AIR FRY, setting the temperature to 400°F, and setting the time to 3 minutes. Select START/STOP to begin.
3. To prepare the chicken wings, cut the wings in half. The meatier part is the drumette. Cut off and

discard the wing tip from the flat part (or save the wing tips in the freezer to make chicken stock).

4. Once the unit is preheated, spray the crisper plate with olive oil. Working in batches, place half the chicken wings into the basket, spray them with olive oil, and sprinkle with the salt and pepper.

5. Select AIR FRY, set the temperature to 400°F, and set the time to 20 minutes. Select START/STOP to begin.

6. After 10 minutes, remove the basket, flip the wings, and spray them with more olive oil. Reinsert the basket to resume cooking.

7. Cook the wings to an internal temperature of 165°F, then transfer them to the bowl with the prepared sauce and toss to coat.

8. Repeat steps 4, 5, 6, and 7 for the remaining chicken wings.

9. Return the coated wings to the basket and air fry for 4 to 6 minutes more until the sauce has glazed the wings and the chicken is crisp. After 3 minutes, check the wings to make sure they aren't burning. Serve hot.

Nutrition: Calories: 913; Total fat: 66g; Saturated fat: 15g; Cholesterol: 244mg; Sodium: 1,722mg; Carbohydrates: 23g; Fiber: 1g; Protein: 59g

Beef Sirloin Roast

Preparation Time: 10 Minutes
Cooking Time: 50 Minutes
Servings: 8

Ingredients:

- 1 tablespoon smoked paprika
- 1 teaspoon ground cumin
- 1 teaspoon garlic powder
- Salt and freshly ground black pepper, to taste
- 2½ pounds sirloin roast

Directions:

1. In a bowl, mix together the spices, salt and black pepper.
2. Rub the roast with spice mixture generously.
3. Place the sirloin roast into the greased baking pan.
4. Press "Power Button" of Ninja Foodi Digital Air Fry Oven and turn the dial to select "Air Roast" mode.
5. Press "Time Button" and again turn the dial to set the cooking time to 50 minutes.
6. Now push "Temp Button" and rotate the dial to set the temperature at 350 degrees F.
7. Press "Start/Pause" button to start.
8. When the unit beeps to show that it is preheated, open the lid and insert baking pan in the oven.
9. When cooking time is complete, open the lid and place the roast onto a platter for about 10 minutes before slicing.
10. With a sharp knife, cut the beef roast into desired sized slices and serve.

Nutrition: Calories: 260 Fat: 11.9g Sat Fat: 4.4g Carbohydrates: 0.4g Fiber: 0.1g Sugar: 0.1g

Bacon-Wrapped Filet Mignon

Preparation Time: 10 Minutes
Cooking Time: 15 Minutes
Servings: 2

Ingredients:
- 2 bacon slices
- 2 (4-ounce) filet mignon
- Salt and freshly ground black pepper, to taste
- Olive oil cooking spray

Directions:
1. Wrap 1 bacon slice around each filet mignon and secure with toothpicks.
2. Season the filets with the salt and black pepper lightly.
3. Press "Power Button" of Ninja Foodi Digital Air Fry Oven and turn the dial to select "Air Fry" mode.
4. Press "Time Button" and again turn the dial to set the cooking time to 15 minutes.
5. Now push "Temp Button" and rotate the dial to set the temperature at 375 degrees F.
6. Press "Start/Pause" button to start.
7. When the unit beeps to show that it is preheated, open the lid.
8. Arrange the filets over the greased rack and insert in the oven.
9. Flip the filets once halfway through.
10. When cooking time is complete, open the lid and transfer the filets onto serving plates.
11. Serve hot.

Nutrition: Calories: 226 Fat: 9.5g Sat Fat: g3.6 Carbohydrates: 0g Fiber: 0g Sugar: 0g Protein: 33.3g

Buttered Rib-Eye Steak

Preparation Time: 10 Minutes
Cooking Time: 14 Minutes
Servings: 3

Ingredients:

- 2 (8-ounce) rib-eye steaks
- 2 tablespoons butter, melted
- Salt and freshly ground black pepper, to taste

Directions:

1. Coat the steak with butter and then sprinkle with salt and black pepper evenly.
2. Press "Power Button" of Ninja Foodi Digital Air Fry Oven and turn the dial to select "Air Roast" mode.
3. Press "Time Button" and again turn the dial to set the cooking time to 14 minutes.
4. Now push "Temp Button" and rotate the dial to set the temperature at 400 degrees F.
5. Press "Start/Pause" button to start.
6. When the unit beeps to show that it is preheated, open the lid and grease the air fry basket.
7. Arrange the steaks into the air fry basket and insert in the oven.
8. When cooking time is complete, open the lid and place steaks onto a platter for about 5 minutes.
9. Cut each steak into desired sized slices and serve.

Nutrition: Calories: 383 Fat: 23.7g Sat Fat: 10.2g Carbohydrates: 0g Fiber: 0g Sugar: 0g Protein: 41g

Spiced Flank Steak

Preparation Time: 10 Minutes
Cooking Time: 12 Minutes
Servings: 6

Ingredients:

- 2 tablespoons balsamic vinegar
- 2 tablespoons olive oil
- 3 garlic cloves, minced
- 1 teaspoon red chili powder
- 1 teaspoon ground cumin
- 1 teaspoon onion powder
- Salt and freshly ground black pepper, to taste
- 1 (2-pound) flank steak

Directions:

1. In a large bowl, mix together the vinegar, spices, salt and black pepper.
2. Add the steak and coat with mixture generously.
3. Cover the bowl and place in the refrigerator for at least 1 hour.
4. Remove the steak from bowl and place onto the greased sheet pan.
5. Press "Power Button" of Ninja Foodi Digital Air Fry Oven and turn the dial to select the "Air Broil" mode.
6. Press "Time Button" and again turn the dial to set the cooking time to 12 minutes.
7. Press "Start/Pause" button to start.
8. When the unit beeps to show that it is preheated, open the lid and insert the sheet pan in the oven.
9. Flip the steak once halfway through.

10. When cooking time is complete, open the lid and place the steak onto a cutting board.
11. With a sharp knife, cut the steak into desired sized slices and serve.

Nutrition: Calories: 341 Fat: 17.4g Sat Fat: 5.9g Carbohydrates: 1.3g Fiber: 0.2g Sugar: 0.2g Protein: 42.3g

Glazed Pork Tenderloin

Preparation Time: 10 Minutes
Cooking Time: 20 Minutes
Servings: 3

Ingredients:

- 2 tablespoons Sriracha
- 2 tablespoons maple syrup
- ¼ teaspoon red pepper flakes, crushed
- Salt, to taste
- 1-pound pork tenderloin

Directions:

1. In a small bowl, add the Sriracha, maple syrup, red pepper flakes and salt and mix well.
2. Brush the pork tenderloin with mixture evenly.
3. Press "Power Button" of Ninja Foodi Digital Air Fry Oven and turn the dial to select "Air Fry" mode.
4. Press "Time Button" and again turn the dial to set the cooking time to 20 minutes.
5. Now push "Temp Button" and rotate the dial to set the temperature at 350 degrees F.
6. Press "Start/Pause" button to start.
7. When the unit beeps to show that it is preheated, open the lid and grease air fry basket.
8. Arrange the pork tenderloin into the air fry basket and insert in the oven.
9. When cooking time is complete, open the lid and place the pork tenderloin onto a platter for about 10 minutes before slicing.
10. With a sharp knife, cut the roast into desired sized slices and serve.

Nutrition: Calories: 261 Fat: 5.4g Sat Fat: 1.8g Carbohydrates: 11g Fiber: 0g Sugar: 8g Protein: 39.6g

SNACKS

Cauliflower with Buffalo Sauce

Preparation time: 5 minutes
Cooking time: 15 minutes
Servings: 6

Ingredients:
- 1 medium head cauliflower, leaves and core removed, cut into bite-sized pieces
- 4 tablespoons salted butter, melted
- ¼ cup dry ranch seasoning
- ¹/₃ cup sugar-free buffalo sauce

Directions:
1. Place cauliflower pieces into a large bowl. Pour butter over cauliflower and toss to coat. Sprinkle in ranch seasoning and toss to coat.
2. Place cauliflower into ungreased air fryer basket. Adjust the temperature to 350°F (180°C) and set the timer for 12 minutes, shaking the basket three times during cooking.
3. When timer beeps, place cooked cauliflower in a clean large bowl. Toss with buffalo sauce, then return to air fryer basket to cook another 3 minutes. Cauliflower bites will be darkened at the edges and tender when done. Serve warm.

Nutrition: calories: 112 fat: 7g protein: 2g carbs: 9g net carbs: 7g fiber: 2g

Cheesy Bacon-Wrapped Jalapeño

Preparation time: 10 minutes
Cooking time: 12 minutes
Servings: 12 poppers

Ingredients:

- 3 ounces (85 g) cream cheese, softened
- $1/_3$ cup shredded mild Cheddar cheese
- ¼ teaspoon garlic powder
- 6 jalapeños (approximately 4-inch long), tops removed, sliced in half lengthwise and seeded
- 12 slices sugar-free bacon

Directions:

1. Place cream cheese, Cheddar, and garlic powder in a large microwave-safe bowl. Microwave 30 seconds on high, then stir. Spoon cheese mixture evenly into hollowed jalapeños.

2. Wrap 1 slice bacon around each jalapeño half, completely covering jalapeño, and secure with a toothpick. Place jalapeños into ungreased air fryer basket. Adjust the temperature to 400°F (205ºC) and set the timer for 12 minutes, turning jalapeños halfway through cooking. Bacon will be crispy when done. Serve warm.

Nutrition: calories: 278 fat: 21g protein: 15g carbs: 3g net carbs: 2g fiber: 1g

Prosciutto Cheese Asparagus Roll

Preparation time: 10 minutes
Cooking time: 10 minutes
Servings: 4
Ingredients:
- 1 pound (454 g) asparagus
- 12 (0.5-ounce 14-g) slices prosciutto
- 1 tablespoon coconut oil, melted
- 2 teaspoons lemon juice
- ⅛ teaspoon red pepper flakes
- $1/_3$ cup grated Parmesan cheese
- 2 tablespoons salted butter, melted

Directions:
1. On a clean work surface, place an asparagus spear onto a slice of prosciutto.
2. Drizzle with coconut oil and lemon juice. Sprinkle red pepper flakes and Parmesan across asparagus. Roll prosciutto around asparagus spear. Place into the air fryer basket.
3. Adjust the temperature to 375°F (190ºC) and set the timer for 10 minutes.
4. Drizzle the asparagus roll with butter before serving.

Nutrition: calories: 263 fat: 20g protein: 14g carbs: 7g net carbs: 4g fiber: 3g

Cheesy Mushroom

Preparation time: 10 minutes
Cooking time: 8 minutes
Servings: 20 mushrooms
Ingredients:
- 4 ounces (113 g) cream cheese, softened
- 6 tablespoons shredded pepper jack cheese
- 2 tablespoons chopped pickled jalapeños
- 20 medium button mushrooms, stems removed
- 2 tablespoons olive oil
- ¼ teaspoon salt
- ⅛ teaspoon ground black pepper

Directions:
1. In a large bowl, mix cream cheese, pepper jack, and jalapeños together.
2. Drizzle mushrooms with olive oil, then sprinkle with salt and pepper. Spoon 2 tablespoons cheese mixture into each mushroom and place in a single layer into ungreased air fryer basket. Adjust the temperature to 370°F (188°C) and set the timer for 8 minutes, checking halfway through cooking to ensure even cooking, rearranging if some are darker than others. When they're golden and cheese is bubbling, mushrooms will be done. Serve warm.

Nutrition: calories: 87 fat: 7g protein: 3g carbs: 2g net carbs: 2g fiber: 0g

Three Cheese Dip

Preparation time: 5 minutes
Cooking time: 12 minutes
Servings: 8
Ingredients:
- 8 ounces (227 g) cream cheese, softened
- ½ cup mayonnaise
- ¼ cup sour cream
- ½ cup shredded sharp Cheddar cheese
- ¼ cup shredded Monterey jack cheese

Directions:
1. In a large bowl, combine all ingredients. Scoop mixture into an ungreased 4-cup nonstick baking dish and place into air fryer basket.
2. Adjust the temperature to 375°F (190ºC) and set the timer for 12 minutes. Dip will be browned on top and bubbling when done. Serve warm.

Nutrition: calories: 245 fat: 23gprotein: 5g carbs: 2g net carbs: 2g fiber: 0g

Cheese Chicken Dip

Preparation time: 10 minutes

Cooking time: 12 minutes

Servings: 8

Ingredients:

- 8 ounces (227 g) cream cheese, softened
- 2 cups chopped cooked chicken thighs
- ½ cup sugar-free buffalo sauce
- 1 cup shredded mild Cheddar cheese, divided

Directions:

1. In a large bowl, combine cream cheese, chicken, buffalo sauce, and ½ cup Cheddar. Scoop dip into an ungreased 4-cup nonstick baking dish and top with remaining Cheddar.
2. Place dish into air fryer basket. Adjust the temperature to 375°F (190ºC) and set the timer for 12 minutes. Dip will be browned on top and bubbling when done. Serve warm.

Nutrition: calories: 222 fat: 15g protein: 14g carbs:1g net carbs: 1g fiber: 0g

Beef and Bacon Cheese Dip

Preparation time: 20 minutes
Cooking time: 10 minutes
Servings: 6

Ingredients:

- 8 ounces (227 g) full-fat cream cheese
- ¼ cup full-fat mayonnaise
- ¼ cup full-fat sour cream
- ¼ cup chopped onion
- 1 teaspoon garlic powder
- 1 tablespoon Worcestershire sauce
- 1¼ cups shredded medium Cheddar cheese, divided
- ½ pound (227g) cooked 80/20 ground beef
- 6 slices sugar-free bacon, cooked and crumbled
- 2 large pickle spears, chopped

Directions:

1. Place cream cheese in a large microwave-safe bowl and microwave for 45 seconds. Stir in mayonnaise, sour cream, onion, garlic powder, Worcestershire sauce, and 1 cup Cheddar. Add cooked ground beef and bacon. Sprinkle remaining Cheddar on top.
2. Place in 6-inch bowl and put into the air fryer basket.
3. Adjust the temperature to 400°F (205ºC) and set the timer for 10 minutes.

4. Dip is done when top is golden and bubbling. Sprinkle pickles over dish. Serve warm.

Nutrition: calories: 457 fat: 35g protein: 22g carbs: 4g net carbs: 3g fiber: 1g

Cheesy Spinach Artichoke Dip

Preparation time: 10 minutes
Cooking time: 10 minutes
Servings: 6

Ingredients:

- 10 ounces (283 g) frozen spinach, drained and thawed
- 1 (14-ounce / 397-g) can artichoke hearts, drained and chopped
- ¼ cup chopped pickled jalapeños
- 8 ounces (227 g) full-fat cream cheese, softened
- ¼ cup full-fat mayonnaise
- ¼ cup full-fat sour cream
- ½ teaspoon garlic powder
- ¼ cup grated Parmesan cheese
- 1 cup shredded pepper jack cheese

Directions:

1. Mix all ingredients in a 4-cup baking bowl. Place into the air fryer basket.
2. Adjust the temperature to 320°F (160ºC) and set the timer for 10 minutes.
3. Remove when brown and bubbling. Serve warm.

Nutrition: calories: 226 fat: 15g protein: 10g carbs: 10g net carbs: 6g fiber: 4g

Cheesy Pizza Crust

Preparation time: 5 minutes
Cooking time: 10 minutes
Servings: 1

Ingredients:

- ½ cup shredded whole-milk Mozzarella cheese
- 2 tablespoons blanched finely ground almond flour
- 1 tablespoon full-fat cream cheese
- 1 large egg white

Directions:

1. Place Mozzarella, almond flour, and cream cheese in a medium microwave-safe bowl. Microwave for 30 seconds. Stir until smooth ball of dough forms. Add egg white and stir until soft round dough forms.
2. Press into a 6-inch round pizza crust.
3. Cut a piece of parchment to fit your air fryer basket and place crust on parchment. Place into the air fryer basket.
4. Adjust the temperature to 350°F (180ºC) and set the timer for 10 minutes.
5. Flip after 5 minutes and at this time place any desired toppings on the crust. Continue cooking until golden. Serve immediately.

Nutrition: calories: 314 fat: 22g protein: 20g carbs: 5g net carbs: 3g fiber: 2g

Sausage and Bacon Cheese Pizza

Preparation time: 5 minutes

Cooking time: 5 minutes

Servings: 1

Ingredients:

- ½ cup shredded Mozzarella cheese
- 7 slices pepperoni
- ¼ cup cooked ground sausage
- 2 slices sugar-free bacon, cooked and crumbled
- 1 tablespoon grated Parmesan cheese
- 2 tablespoons low-carb, sugar-free pizza sauce, for dipping

Directions:

1. Cover the bottom of a 6-inch cake pan with Mozzarella. Place pepperoni, sausage, and bacon on top of cheese and sprinkle with Parmesan. Place pan into the air fryer basket.
2. Adjust the temperature to 400°F (205ºC) and set the timer for 5 minutes.
3. Remove when cheese is bubbling and golden. Serve warm with pizza sauce for dipping.

Nutrition: calories: 466 fat: 34g protein: 28g carbs: 5g net carbs: 4g fiber: 1g

DESSERTS

Buttery Fennel and Garlic

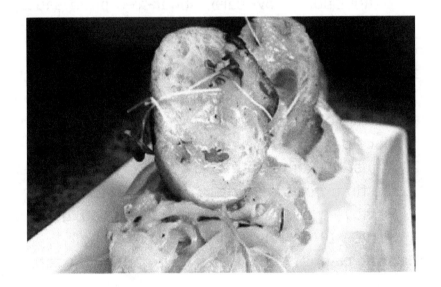

Preparation Time: 10 Minutes
Cooking Time: 5 Minutes
Servings: 4

Ingredients:

- ½ stick butter
- 2 garlic cloves, sliced
- ½ teaspoon salt
- 1 and ½ pounds fennel bulbs, cut into wedges
- ¼ teaspoon ground black pepper
- ½ teaspoon cayenne
- ¼ teaspoon dried dill weed
- 1/3 cup dry white wine
- 2/3 cup stock

Directions:

1. Set your Ninja Foodi Deluxe to Sauté mode and add butter, let it heat up
2. Add garlic and cook for 30 seconds
3. Add rest of the ingredients
4. Lock lid & cook on LOW pressure for 3 minutes
5. Remove lid and serve
6. Enjoy!

Nutrition: Calories: 111 Fat: 6g Saturated Fat: 2 g Carbohydrates: 2 g Fiber: 2 g Sodium: 317 mg Protein: 2 g

Simple Poached Pears

Preparation Time: 5 Minutes
Cooking Time: 10 Minutes
Servings: 6
Ingredients:
- 6 firm pears, peeled
- 4 garlic cloves, minced
- 1 stick cinnamon
- 1 fresh ginger, minced
- 1 bottle of dry red wine
- 1 bay leaf
- Mixed Italian herbs as needed
- 1 and 1/3 cups stevia

Directions:
1. Peel the pears leaving the stems attached
2. Pour wine into your Ninja Foodi Deluxe
3. Add cinnamon, cloves, and ginger, bay leaf, and stevia, stir gently
4. Add pears to the pot
5. Close the lid
6. Cook for 9 minutes on HIGH
7. Quickly release the pressure
8. Take the pears out using a tong, keep them on the side
9. Set Sauté mode, make the mixture into half
10. Drizzle the mixture with pears
11. Serve and enjoy!

Nutrition: Calories: 150 Fat: 16g Saturated Fat: 4 g Carbohydrates: 2g Fiber: 0 g Sodium: 13 mg Protein: 0.5g

Cheesy Cauliflower Steak

Preparation Time: 10 Minutes
Cooking Time: 30 Minutes
Servings: 4
Ingredients:
- 1 tablespoon mustard
- 1 head cauliflower
- 1 teaspoon avocado mayonnaise
- ½ cup parmesan cheese, grated
- ¼ cup butter, cut into small pieces

Directions:
1. Set your Ninja Foodi Deluxe to Sauté mode and add butter and cauliflower
2. Sauté for 3 minutes
3. Add remaining ingredients and stir
4. Lock lid and then cook on HIGH pressure for about 25-30 minutes
5. Release pressure naturally over 10 minutes
6. Serve and enjoy!

Nutrition: Calories: 155 Fat: 13g Saturated Fat: 2 g Carbohydrates: 4 g Fiber: 2 g Sodium: 162 mg Protein: 6 g

Garlic and Mushroom Munchies

Preparation Time: 10 Minutes
Cooking Time: 8 Minutes
Servings: 4

Ingredients:

- ¼ cup vegetable stock
- 2 tablespoons extra virgin olive oil
- 1 tablespoon Dijon mustard
- 1 teaspoon dried thyme
- 1 teaspoon of sea salt
- ½ teaspoon dried rosemary
- ¼ teaspoon fresh ground black pepper
- 2 pounds cremini mushrooms, cleaned
- 6 garlic cloves, minced
- ¼ cup fresh parsley, chopped

Directions:

1. Take a small bowl and whisk in vegetable stock, mustard, olive oil, salt, thyme, pepper and rosemary
2. Add mushrooms, garlic and stock mix to your Ninja Foodi Deluxe
3. Close lid and cook on SLOW COOK Mode (LOW) for 8 hours
4. Open the lid and stir in parsley
5. Serve and enjoy!

Nutrition: Calories: 92 Fat: 5g Saturated Fat: 2 g Carbohydrates: 8 g Fiber: 2 g Sodium: 550 mg Protein: 4 g

Warm Glazed Up Carrots

Preparation Time: 5 Minutes
Cooking Time: 5 Minutes
Servings: 4
Ingredients:
- 2 pounds carrots
- Pepper as needed
- 1 cup of water
- 1 tablespoon coconut butter

Directions:
1. Wash carrots thoroughly & peel then, slice the carrots
2. Add carrots, water to the Ninja Foodi Deluxe
3. Lock pressure lid & cook for 4 minutes on HIGH pressure
4. Release pressure naturally
5. Strain carrots and strain carrots
6. Mix with coconut butter, enjoy with a bit of pepper

Nutrition: Calories: 228 Fat: 8g Saturated Fat: 2 g Carbohydrates: 36g Fiber: 2 g Sodium: 123 mg Protein: 4g

Decadent Lemon Mousse

Preparation Time: 10 Minutes
Cooking Time: 12 Minutes
Servings: 2

Ingredients:

- 1-2 ounces cream cheese, soft
- ½ teaspoon lemon liquid stevia
- ½ cup heavy cream
- 1/8 cup fresh lemon juice
- 2 pinch salt

Directions:

1. In a bowl add heavy cream, cream cheese, stevia, lemon juice and salt
2. Pour the mixture into a ramekin and transfer to Ninja Foodi Deluxe
3. Close the lid
4. Set Bake/Roast mode
5. Bake for 12 minutes to 350-degree F
6. Check the doneness it before remove from the Ninja Foodi Deluxe
7. Serve and enjoy!

Nutrition: Calories: 292 Fat: 26g Saturated Fat: 8 g Carbohydrates: 8g Fiber: 1 g Sodium: 30 mg Protein: 5g

Pumpkin Carrot Pudding

Preparation Time: 10 Minutes
Cooking Time: 20 Minutes
Servings: 2

Ingredients:

- 2 cups pumpkin, pureed
- 2 cups carrots, shredded
- 2 whole eggs
- 1 tablespoon granulated Erythritol
- 1 teaspoon ground nutmeg
- 1 tablespoon extra-virgin olive oil
- ½ sweet onion, finely chopped
- 1 cup heavy whip cream
- ½ cup cream cheese, soft
- ¼ cup pumpkin seeds, garnish
- ¼ cup water
- ½ teaspoon salt

Directions:

1. Add oil to your Ninja Foodi Deluxe and whisk in pumpkin, carrots, heavy cream, cream cheese, eggs, erythritol, onion, nutmeg, water and salt
2. Stir gently and close the lid
3. Cook for 10 minutes on HIGH
4. Release pressure naturally over 10 minutes
5. Top with the pumpkin seeds
6. Serve and enjoy!

Nutrition: Calories: 239 Fat: 19g Saturated Fat: 4 g Carbohydrates: 7g Fiber: 2 g Sodium: 423 mg Protein: 6g

Awesome Poached Pears

Preparation Time: 5 Minutes
Cooking Time: 10 Minutes
Servings: 6

Ingredients:

- 6 firm pears, peeled
- 4 garlic cloves, minced
- 1 stick cinnamon
- 1 fresh ginger, minced
- 1 bottle of dry red wine
- 1 bay leaf
- Mixed Italian herbs as needed
- 1 and 1/3 cups stevia

Directions:

1. Peel the pears leaving the stems attached
2. Pour wine into your Ninja Foodi Deluxe
3. Add cinnamon, cloves, ginger, bay leaf and stevia, stir gently
4. Add pears to the pot
5. Close the lid
6. Cook for 9 minutes on HIGH
7. Quickly release the pressure
8. Take the pears out using a tong, keep them on the side
9. Set Sauté mode, make the mixture into half
10. Drizzle the mixture with pears
11. Serve and enjoy!

Nutrition: Calories: 150 Fat: 16g Saturated Fat: 4 g Carbohydrates: 2g Fiber: 0 g Sodium: 13 mg Protein: 0.5g

Spiced Baked Apple and Homemade Apple Spice

Preparation Time: 5 Minutes
Cooking Time: 10 Minutes
Servings: 4
Ingredients:
- 4 smalls to medium-sized apples
- 2 tablespoons coconut oil
- 2 tablespoons sugar
- 2 tablespoons ground cinnamon
- 2 teaspoons ground nutmeg
- 1 ½ teaspoons allspice

Directions:
1. Homemade Apple Spice:
2. In a medium bowl, mix cinnamon, nutmeg, and allspice.
3. Pour into a small air-tight container.
4. Shake well to make sure the spice is well mixed.
5. Wash, peel, and slice the apples into rounds. Place them in a bowl.
6. Melt the coconut oil in a small saucepan on the stove.
7. Drizzle melted coconut oil over the sliced apples.
8. Sprinkle the apples with homemade apple spice and sugar.
9. Use a spoon to stir the apples to make sure the spice and coconut oil covers all the apple slices.

10. Use non-stick cooking spray to spray the cake pan.
11. Preheat the Air Fryer to 350°F or 180°Celsius (C). Use the Air Fry setting and set the Preheat for 3 minutes.
12. Place the apple slices in the cake pan.
13. Place the cake pan in the preheated Air Fryer.
14. Set the Air Fryer for 10 minutes and use the Air Fry setting to start baking the apple slices.
15. At 5 minutes, pause the Air Fryer, open the Air Fryer draw to check and turn the apple slices.
16. Start the Air Fryer to cook the apples for the last 5 minutes.
17. After 10 minutes, the Air Fryer will switch off. The apples should be cooked through.
18. Once the apples are cooked, remove the Air Fryer drawer and place it on the cooling rack or mat.
19. Remove the cake pan from the air fryer, use oven gloves.
20. Divide into portions and serve.

Nutrition: 199 Calories 37.1g Carbs 29.2g Sugars 0.6g Protein 7.3g Fat 5.5g Fiber

Sugar Dough Dippers

Preparation Time: 17 Minutes
Cooking Time: 8 Minutes
Servings: 4

Ingredients:

- 1 teaspoon white sugar
- 2 cups all-purpose flour
- ¼ teaspoon baking soda
- ½ teaspoon baking powder
- 1 flat teaspoon salt
- 4 tablespoons butter
- 1/2 cup buttermilk
- 2 tablespoons whole fresh milk

Directions:

1. In a bowl, sieve together 1 ½ cups of flour, salt, baking soda, and baking powder.
2. Put 1 tablespoon of the butter aside.
3. Use the rest of the butter to rub into the flour mix to make a crumbling mixture.
4. Pour the buttermilk into the flour mixture, stir with a cake spatula until the mixture turns into dough. Do not over mix, you want it to be a nice manageable dough texture.
5. Clean a working surface and sprinkle some flour over it. This is where you are going to cut out the biscuits from the dough.
6. Manipulate the dough into a round shape that is at least ½ inch thick.
7. Use a round cookie-cutter that is not too large, cut out 10 round dough shapes.
8. Use non-stick cooking spray to spray the Air Fryer drawer.

9. Line the Air Fryer drawer with Air Fryer parchment paper.

10. Preheat the Air Fryer to 400°F. Use the Air Fry setting and set the Preheat for 3 minutes.

11. Melt the last block of butter in a small saucepan on the stovetop.

12. Brush the cookies with the melted butter.

13. Place the cookies in the Air Fryer. Do not crowd and only use one layer to fill the Air Fryer drawer.

14. Set the Air Fryer for 8 minutes and use the Air Fry setting to start cooking the dessert.

15. After 8 minutes, the Air Fryer will switch off. The dough balls should be golden brown and cooked through.

16. Once the dough dippers are cooked, remove the Air Fryer drawer and place it on the cooling rack or mat.

17. Remove the dough dippers by using the spatula or food tongs.

18. Divide into portions and serve.

Nutrition: 469 calories 77.7g carbs 12.1g sugars 10.6g protein 12.8g fat 2.4g fiber

CONCLUSION

Here are some more tips for you:

How to Properly Clean and Store Your Air Fryer

The key to keeping your around for years to come is to make sure that it is properly taken care of. The machine is nice because most of its parts are dishwasher safe, but to extend the life of your machine it is always best to hand wash it. Here are a few tips for cleaning and storing your air fryer:

1. Always make sure that your machine is unplugged and the elements are at room temperature before cleaning.
2. Prepping can get messy if you need to clean the outside of your machine wipe down the outside with a damp towel.
3. The pan and basket should be cleaned with hot soapy water and a non-abrasive, non-metal sponge. Feel free to soak the pan and basket in hot soapy water if there is any stuck-on food.
4. Wipe down the inside of the machine with a damp towel.
5. Use a soft scrub brush to clean the heating element of any food residues.
6. Store your machine in a cool, dry place to prevent unnecessary wear and dust build up.

How to Properly Store Foods

1. Let Them Cool Before Storing

Storing food that is still warm causes condensation to build up inside the container which leads to soft and moist foods. Let the food cool for as long as possible before putting in a container. You can also pierce small holes in the top of the storage containers to allow anymore condensation to release.

2. Store Baked Goods in Paper or Plastic Wrap

People have been using paper bags to store stuff for decades, the more notable thing here is that you can use an air fryer to make baked goods. Whether you are cooking a traditional cake or even making donuts, they can be stored for long periods of time in brown paper or plastic wrap to maintain their freshness.

3. Freeze them in Storage Bags

Once your food is properly cooled, you should put it in a freezer bag and get out as much air as possible before freezing it. When you are ready to reheat your food, let it thaw and then put it back in your fryer to reheat it. It will not have the same crispness as fresh out of the fryer food, but it will retain a little crispness and all of the flavor.

4. Wrap it in Foil

If you absolutely need to store food without an adequate cooling time, the best way to store it is by wrapping it in tin foil. The foil will draw some of the heat out to keep it from creating condensation and making the food soggy. Foil works to keep the food ready to serve in minutes or days which makes it one of the best options for fried food period.

Safety Concerns When Using Your Air Fryer

Traditional fryers and air fryers surprisingly share the same safety concerns, though in slightly different ways. Both can cause burns and smoke, though an oil-less fryer is inherently safer than a traditional oil fryer. You should never leave your air fryer alone for too long while you are cooking because you never know what could happen. These machines are relatively safe, but it is always better to be safe than sorry with any appliance.

Once again, thank you and enjoy.

CPSIA information can be obtained
at www.ICGtesting.com
Printed in the USA
BVHW092110200421
605421BV00004B/115

9 781801 752381